DISCOVERING THE CARROT EFFECT

The art of successful problem solving

DR. LEE GRUNER

USA ▪ Canada ▪ UK ▪ Ireland

Note for Librarians: A cataloguing record for this book is available from Library and Archives
Canada at www.collectionscanada.ca/amicus/index-e.html
ISBN 1-4120-6751-0

*Printed on paper with minimum 30% recycled fibre. Trafford's print shop
runs on "green energy" from solar, wind and other environmentally-friendly power sources.*

TRAFFORD

Offices in Canada, USA, Ireland and UK
This book was published *on-demand* in cooperation with Trafford Publishing. On-demand
publishing is a unique process and service of making a book available for retail sale to the
public taking advantage of on-demand manufacturing and Internet marketing. On-demand
publishing includes promotions, retail sales, manufacturing, order fulfilment, accounting and
collecting royalties on behalf of the author.

Book sales for North America and international:
Trafford Publishing, 6E–2333 Government St.,
Victoria, BC v8t 4p4 CANADA
phone 250 383 6864 (toll-free 1 888 232 4444)
fax 250 383 6804; email to orders@trafford.com
Book sales in Europe:
Trafford Publishing (uk) Ltd., Enterprise House, Wistaston Road Business Centre,
Wistaston Road, Crewe, Cheshire cw2 7rp UNITED KINGDOM
phone 01270 251 396 (local rate 0845 230 9601)
facsimile 01270 254 983; orders.uk@trafford.com
Order online at:
trafford.com/05-1662

10 9 8 7 6 5 4 3

Table of Contents

Introduction

We talk a lot about "people being unable to see the wood for the trees." What does this really mean? Basically it means that someone is so focused on something in front of their nose that they can't see the bigger picture. A well-known example is the three blind men and the elephant all of whom described the elephant according to the part that they could touch.

I have noticed that it is common for individuals to pose what they believe is a problem, but that what they are actually doing is putting forward "their" solution. They haven't determined what the actual problem really is and haven't considered that putting in place their solution is more than likely to cause problems for other people and/or only address part of what the underlying problem really is.

Often in this high paced world of ours we spend minimal time on the things that will deliver us a problem solved for the longer term and take the easiest approach, an approach that appears on the surface to be time efficient. In addition, we may take what seems to be the obvious solution without considering all of the ramifications or exploring the options that may lead to a far better solution for the longer term—a solution that will provide the best outcomes for everyone impacted by the problem.

And so we are doomed to have our problem arise again and again and to spend time again and again not solving the problem but responding to what appears to be "the solution." Rather than save time, we waste time and all because we didn't put the effort in up front to understand what the problem really was and then try to get the best solution using a practical team based process.

One of the major barriers to successful problem solving is lack of perspective and inability or unwillingness to identify options.

The story of Rominy Rabbit, the rabbit who hated carrots, is an example of how to successfully solve complex problems and will provide the key factors that will assist anyone in any organisation or sphere of life to ensure problems are successfully identified and feasible solutions put in place.

In my working day, I frequently meet Rominy Rabbits. I am sure each of you also knows many Rominy Rabbits and that you continue to be endlessly frustrated in your relationships with them. I have learnt how to work with different Rominy Rabbits and even Rominy Rabbits en masse to overcome shortsightedness and achieve successful outcomes with a minimum of fuss. I hope that this little book will assist you to work successfully with your own Rominy Rabbits.

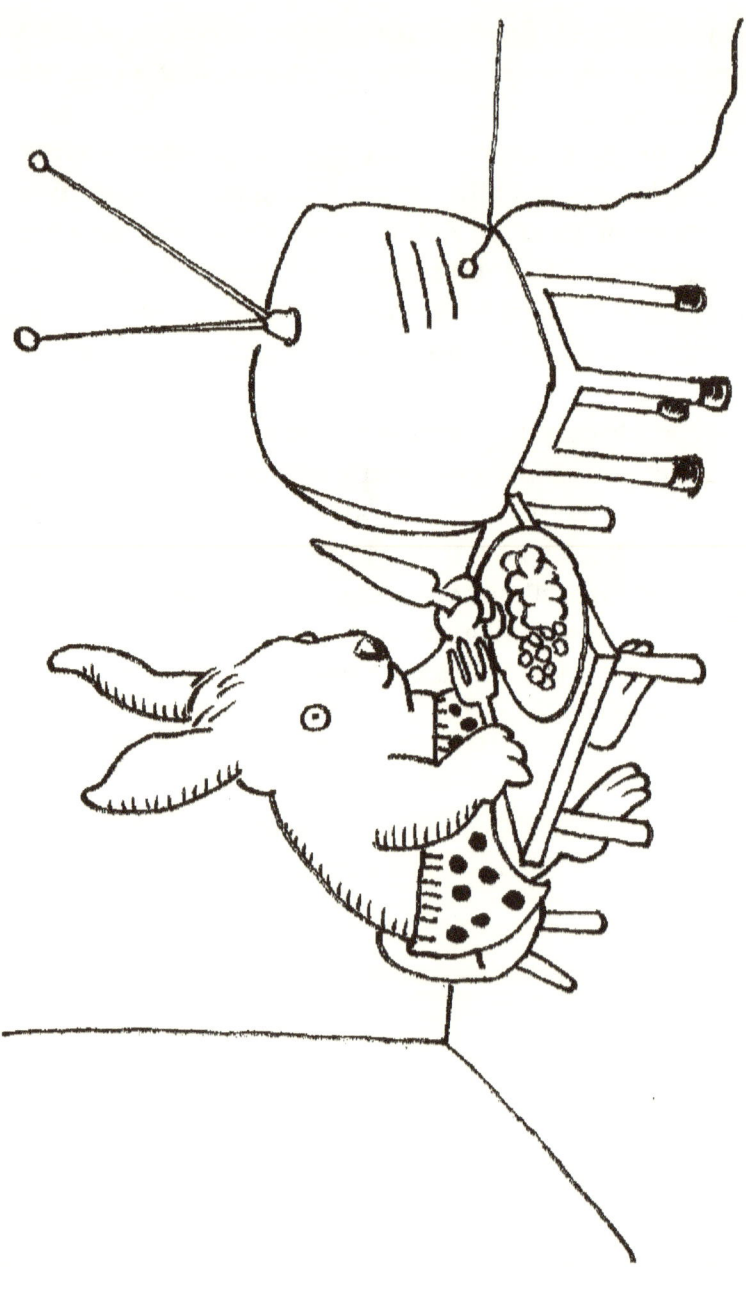

Rominy Rabbit could only see what was right in front of his nose

The Rabbit Who Hated Carrots

Who ever heard of a rabbit that hated carrots? After all, carrots are a rabbit's staple diet. Just think of Bugs Bunny, Peter Rabbit or any other famous rabbit you know. They virtually lived on carrots- it's a wonder they didn't become orange, like humans tend to do if they eat too many.

Rominy Rabbit is nowhere near as famous, but he does deserve his place in history. Without Rominy Rabbit, the Carrot Effect would never have been discovered. And if the Carrot Effect had never been discovered it would have meant the end of the Happy Valley Rabbit Community.

Rominy Rabbit loathed carrots. He seemed to have an aversion to anything sweet and carrots especially brought him out in spots. His mother first discovered this very early in Rominy's life and luckily changed his diet. Rominy grew large and cuddly and very handsome, but he had one major problem. He was very short sighted.

Of course, being a rabbit, no one had diagnosed this problem and Rominy thought his eyesight was normal. It is hard to miss what you have never had, so Rominy thought seeing things in a blur unless they were at the tip of your nose, was quite normal and that all other rabbits were the same as he was. He felt healthy and strong. He could run fast and jump and he couldn't see

Every day Walter Rabbit would sit on the tree stump and help rabbits solve their problems

anything wrong with a carrot free diet. When he was very young, and other rabbits pointed things out to him that were far away, he thought they had good imaginations and he imagined things too and agreed with the other rabbits. However as he grew older, his imagination grew less vivid and he ceased to agree with the other rabbits. If he couldn't see what they saw, then it wasn't there, and he said so.

The other rabbits found Rominy very difficult to get along with and he had a reputation for only seeing things one way and never being prepared to show some perspective. Even though he had two good eyes, the other rabbits considered him a one eyed rabbit and nicknamed him "one-eye". This made Rominy even more difficult as he **knew** he was right- surely he should be able to trust what was right in front of his eyes?

The Happy Valley Rabbit Community was led by Walter Rabbit, a wise old brown bunny with a chewed left ear resulting from a fight with a large dog many years before. Walter Rabbit was highly respected by the whole rabbit clan and the only rabbit that Rominy also respected. Every day between 10 am and 12 noon Walter took his place on an old tree stump on the edge of the Great Green Forest and dealt with the problems brought to him by the members of the rabbit clan. The problems were wide and varied.

"Mr Farmer has fenced off his vegetable patch, how can we ensure our carrot supply for winter?"

"Baby Rabbit will not listen to my advice and keeps running away over the fields where there is a large dog".

"I think I saw a fox yesterday, what should I do?"

Walter Rabbit would think through all of the questions. Some he would answer immediately. Others he would take on notice and reply the next day. If some of the problems were particularly complex, Walter would set up a team to develop solutions.

Sometimes, rabbits would come to Walter with solutions rather than problems.

"Walter, we need a bigger plot."

"Walter, you need to move Jenny Rabbit and her children to the next field".

This required more effort for Walter.

"First you need to identify the problem" he would say. "You have given me a solution, but what is the problem?"

This meant that he needed to work with the particular rabbit to try and elucidate what the problem was. This often took some time as the rabbit could not always understand the problem, but generally they were able to sort this out together and then develop solutions.

Rominy Rabbit was a major problem for Walter. Rominy Rabbit **never** came with problems. He **always** came with solutions. And no matter what Walter did, he just couldn't get Rominy to see that underlying the solution there was actually a problem.

"Walter, I want you stop people calling me one eye"

"Walter, I deserve more lettuces, because I don't eat carrots"

"Walter, you must ensure that I get my holidays in December."

Often Walter gave in to Rominy, much against his better judgement because this was the only way to get Rominy to stop hassling him and taking up his time. Naturally the other rabbits saw this as favouritism.

Walter Rabbit knew that this situation could not continue indefinitely as it was already causing disruption in the rabbit community. He needed to take some action. The question was what and how?

He thought again about what it was that made Rominy so different from the other rabbits. Why was it that he had absolutely no perspective and seemed quite unable to learn? The only thing that he could come up with after many times assessing the problem was Rominy's diet. It must be something to do with carrots, but how to prove this?

Walter Rabbit was a great believer in data. He did not believe in assumption, as that was where you were most likely to make mistakes. So he decided that he would collect some data on carrots and perspective to see whether his hypothesis had any substance. He gathered some of the younger rabbits and engaged them in the task.

"I want you to help me do some research," he said. "I would like each of you to interview 10 rabbits and write down how many carrots they are eating each day and then to test their eyesight by using this chart". He provided clear instructions on where to place the chart and the distance the chart was to be from the subject. Each rabbit was provided with a check sheet to record the information.

One week later, Walter Rabbit had all of the check sheets and sat down to collate them into a graph- carrots per day on the horizontal axis and visual acuity on the vertical axis. The results he obtained both amazed and shocked him. There was a direct correlation up to 5 carrots a day, then visual acuity remained the same for those with more than 5 carrots per day. He noted that no rabbit other than Rominy ate less than 2 carrots per day. Rominy with no carrots per day had a far lower visual acuity than any other rabbit. No wonder he had no perspective! He could just barely see things that were in front of his nose.

The other thing that Walter Rabbit noticed was that the rabbits with the lower visual acuity were the ones most likely to come to him with solutions rather than problems. Walter Rabbit could hardly believe the enormous power of eating carrots. However, the problem still remained that Rominy could not eat carrots, so there was no way of improving the situation. Unless somehow, there was a way of reproducing the influence of carrots- discovering **the Carrot Effect**. The Carrot Effect could be used as a tool to develop perspective and enhance problem solving in myopic rabbits. If he could only find the Carrot Effect, he could at last make Rominy see the big picture.

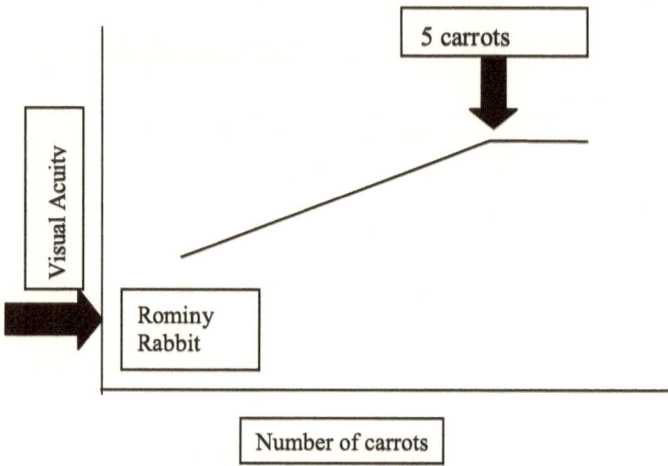

Walter Rabbit decided to collect some more data, this time specifically on Rominy. He talked to Rominy's parents and his brothers and sisters and he compiled a list of Likes and Dislikes.

Likes
- Singing
- Turnips
- Lettuce
- Mathematical equations
- Poetry
- Rosemary Rabbit

Dislikes
- Carrots ++++
- Apples
- Dogs
- Sweet corn
- Games
- Winter

Walter Rabbit was not quite sure how he would use this information, but he stored the list away in his Rominy file- just in case.

Walter Rabbit Defines The Problem

Walter Rabbit packed a knapsack with carrots, lettuce, apples, his Rominy file, a clean tee shirt and some clean underwear. He told his wife Amelia Rabbit that he needed some time to think through this problem and might be away for a week. He made his way into the Great Green Forest where he had established his favourite thinking place and a snug little burrow for sleeping.

Walter Rabbit sat under a venerable old oak and in his mind tossed around, turnips, lettuce, singing, poetry, Rosemary Rabbit, mathematical equations until they all blended into one big orange "carrot effect". The Carrot Effect had a nebulous shape and seemed to float in the air. What was it? Where was it? How could he find it? How would he use it?

For five days Walter Rabbit sat, trying to get the Carrot Effect to reveal itself, but he had no success. That night he went to bed in his burrow, quite despondent. There seemed to be no way to decide what to do. The next morning he woke up re-energised. "I need to start with first principles," he said to himself, "just like I do when I work with the other rabbits on their problems. I need to make a list". So he took a fresh sheet of paper out of his Rominy file and wrote down:

Problem = Current Situation – Desired Situation

Current Situation: all the things that are happening now that I would like to change

Desired Situation: the outcome that would make me happy

What Is the Current Situation?

➢ A rabbit who cannot see past his nose
➢ A rabbit who causes disruption because he cannot see past his nose
➢ Dissatisfaction in the rabbit community as Rominy disagrees with everyone and often gets his way
➢ Rominy's way is rarely what is best for the other rabbits
➢ We are not doing the right thing
➢ I am stressed trying to deal with the situation
➢ Over time the situation is bound to undermine my authority

What Is The Desired Situation?

➢ Rominy Rabbit gains some perspective
➢ I am able to do the right thing by the rabbit community on all occasions
➢ I reduce my own stress
➢ Rominy and the other rabbits live together harmoniously (as much as possible)

Problem Definition

Rominy's lack of perspective is causing disruption in the rabbit clan and hinders decisions being made for the good of all

Walter Rabbit looked at the sheet. It was true that he was no nearer to discovering The Carrot Effect, but he felt a lot better. He felt that he had achieved something. Being an analytical rabbit, he evaluated why he felt better.

"Well', he said to himself," I can use this problem definition to work with a team to progress a solution". Walter had a great belief in teams. He knew that if you got the right team together, you could solve complex problems far more effectively than you could on your own. So Walter Rabbit made another list, a list of possible team members:

> - Jenny Rabbit: mother of 12 and an incredible organiser
> - Fluffy Bunny: a younger rabbit known for his spirit of adventure and innovative ideas
> - Reginald Rabbit: an old grumpy rabbit, good on detail and with a negative bent
> - Serena Rabbit: a sociable rabbit who could get information out of a stone
> - Quentin Rabbit: talented at jigsaw puzzles

Walter Rabbit was convinced that with this team he would find the Carrot Effect and would work out how best to use it. By this time it was evening. He took out the last of his carrots and a little lettuce to eat for his dinner. Then he crawled into his burrow to sleep. Tomorrow he would go home.

Walter Rabbit
Goes Home

Walter woke early and packed his knapsack. He ate his last remaining apple for breakfast as he walked through the Great Green Forest with a spring in his step. As he walked, he thought about the team that he had chosen and how he would engage them in the task. Other than Reginald Rabbit who had recently retired from his position as gardener of the main plot, all of the other rabbits had very busy lives and they would need to see The Quest as very important to get involved. The Quest was likely to take considerable time and cause some disruption.

"What is the best way to engage them," thought Walter, "and of course each one will be different. Jenny Rabbit has 12 children and some of them are still quite young. She will be reluctant to leave them. I need to get over that reluctance and find someone willing to look after her family. What would appeal to Jenny Rabbit and make her want to join The Quest?"

Walter knew that Jenny Rabbit had an innate sense of responsibility. Even though she had such a large family, she was always helping others less fortunate than herself and she was always ready to join committees that would help the community. However, this never involved leaving her family, so The Quest needed to be painted in such a way that this would overcome all obstacles. Walter felt that the problems of the future would be enough to capture Jenny's imagination as these would impact on her own children.

He wondered if his wife Amelia Rabbit would be prepared to care for Jenny's family with the help of Joanna Rabbit next door. That would be a good solution. Now he just had to get Amelia on side. Walter smiled to himself. After many years of marriage, he knew just how to do that!

So how was he to get Fluffy Bunny on board? Fluffy Bunny had just started a part time job at The Big Bunny Café and Walter Rabbit knew that Fluffy Bunny loved his work and the financial independence it brought him. But Walter Rabbit also knew that there was one thing that Fluffy Bunny valued even more than his work and that was being valued and respected in the community. Being such a young rabbit, he was still trying to earn this respect. Walter Rabbit knew that if The Quest was successful, this would earn Fluffy Bunny the respect he craved. In addition, Fluffy Bunny had a very strong spirit of adventure and tended to get into mischief. This would be a way of using his adventurousness for the good of the community.

Of course there was a risk that The Quest would not be successful, but Fluffy Bunny was a risk taker and Walter Rabbit felt that this would not be an issue. Walter sighed, of course he would also need to speak to the owner of the Big Bunny Café and not only get his support to release Fluffy Bunny from his duties, but also to ensure that Fluffy Bunny got his job back on his return.

Reginald Rabbit had time to go on The Quest, but Reginald Rabbit was not an easy target. He could be grumpy and cantankerous and very negative. He also had arthritis in his knees and could not run fast or jump far. Even if he was willing to get involved, he was likely to find the physical part of The Quest a trial. Reginald Rabbit would be by far the most difficult to convince that The Quest was worthwhile.

Walter Rabbit was still thinking about this when he emerged from the Great Green Forest and entered the path in the fields that would take him home. As he looked about him and squinted in the bright sunlight, a voice assailed his ears. "Walter Rabbit, where have you been? You need to tell Farmer Rabbit to give me more turnips". And there was Rominy Rabbit, large as life, doing what he always did. If ever Walter Rabbit knew that The Quest was the right thing to do, this was the time! "Rominy, I have just come out of the Great Green Forest. I am tired, hungry and desperately need a wash. I cannot deal with anything until I have done this and seen my wife Amelia Rabbit. I will talk to you tomorrow." "But!" said Rominy Rabbit. Walter Rabbit strode on without looking back.

He couldn't help but smile as he approached his own front door as there outside, swathed in a large apron was Amelia Rabbit sweeping the front step. She had her back to Walter Rabbit, but something must have warned her that he was near and she turned and his smile was reflected on her face. "I have missed you Walter Rabbit," she said. "You look a bit tired and grubby, I will run you a bath right away." "Just before you do," Walter Rabbit said. His arms went around her and he hugged her with all his might. There was nothing better than coming home.

Half an hour later, Walter Rabbit soaked in the large bathtub, thinking of nothing. While the Great Green Forest was the place to do serious thinking, the bath was the place to completely clear his head and lazily wash. The only thought in his head was how wonderful it was to be home and how glorious it was to lie in the bath doing nothing. Walter Rabbit spent a whole hour in the bath, filling up with more hot water every now and then. When he got out, he noticed that Amelia Rabbit had put out his favourite dressing gown and his fluffy slippers and as he put these on, he became aware of the most delectable smell. Home made carrot soup with parsnip and parsley- his absolute favourite!

It wasn't until he had finished his soup that Walter Rabbit

began to share his thoughts with Amelia Rabbit. He respected her opinion greatly. She was not only his wife, but also his support, his mentor and his severest critic. Between the two of them they would sort out the right approach. Walter Rabbit shared his thought processes and how he had come to his conclusion about The Quest. He discussed his team and his initial thoughts about getting the team members enthused. Amelia Rabbit asked questions to clarify the issues, but overall believed that this was the way to go.

"Have you worked out how to get Reginald Rabbit involved?" she asked, "No", replied Walter Rabbit. "I think it might be quite difficult". "Why don't you let me do the enthusing," said Amelia Rabbit. "You know he has always had a soft spot for me, ever since I sat on his knee as a small bunny and made him laugh." "That's true," replied Walter Rabbit. "If anyone can get Reginald Rabbit to do anything, it is you. And we have to remember that Reginald Rabbit is grumpier than ever because he feels he has lost his goal in life now that he has retired. The Quest for The Carrot Effect will give him a new goal." "What about looking after Jenny Rabbit's family? Do you think you and Joanna Rabbit could manage that?" Amelia agreed that she would talk to Joanna Rabbit and they would sort out the logistics between them.

There were only Serena and Quentin Rabbit to consider and a discussion between Walter and Amelia Rabbit sorted out how to get them on side. Quentin Rabbit was looking for acknowledgement that doing jigsaw puzzles was a valuable way to use his time. Walter Rabbit felt that it was just this skill of identifying pieces and where they fitted that was needed for The Quest and if it was successful, Quentin Rabbit's passion would at last be vindicated.

Serena Rabbit on the other hand was viewed by many of the Rabbit Clan as a bit of a flibbertigibbet, decorative but useless. Walter Rabbit had had many discussions with her and knew that this impression was totally unjust. Hidden under the outgoing, creative, fun-loving exterior was a highly intelligent and somewhat intellectual rabbit, who would not only keep the team amused, but would offer sound advice. Serena Rabbit had an opportunity to establish a high reputation by being part of The Quest.

After their discussion, Amelia Rabbit looked a bit thoughtful. "What is still bothering you?" asked Walter Rabbit. "Well," said Amelia Rabbit, "The Quest will have an impact not only on the team, but also on the whole rabbit community. You need to get the families and the employers of the team on side. We don't want them to come back to unhappy partners or lose their jobs. You really will need to tell them why The Quest for The Carrot Effect is important and let them have some input. I know they respect you greatly, but the Happy Valley Rabbit Community shouldn't be asked to take this all on trust. In addition, you may be away for some time and you will need to find a replacement for the tree stump sessions. The community should have a say in who that replacement should be." Walter Rabbit said nothing for a while, then slowly nodded his head. "And I will need to speak to Rominy Rabbit too," he said.

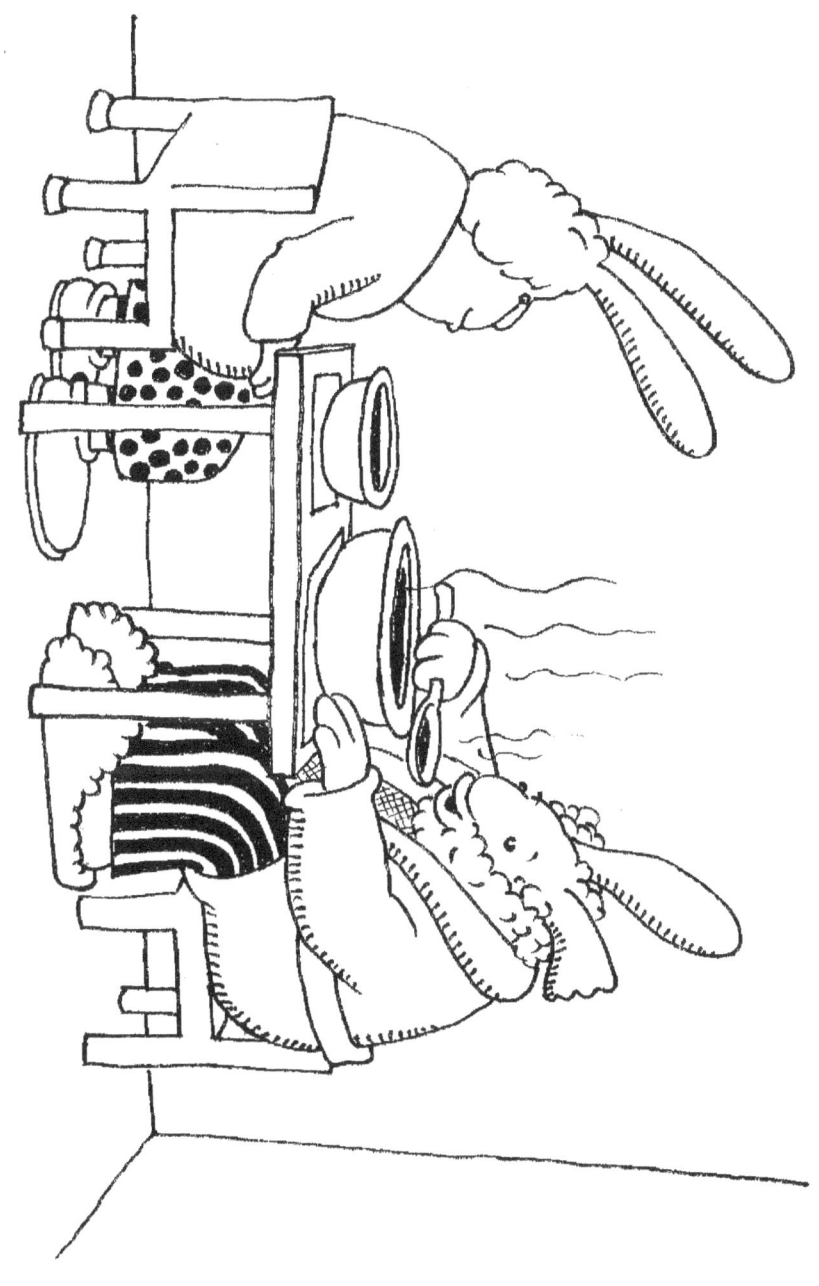

Walter Rabbit always consulted with Amelia Rabbit on difficult issues

The Community Provides Its Support

The next few weeks flew by. Walter Rabbit assembled his team with the help of Amelia Rabbit and was gratified that all team members agreed to be part of The Quest. He asked Fluffy Bunny to prepare posters announcing the community meeting and put them up in a variety of locations where they would be seen by all the rabbits:

Community Meeting
All Rabbits Invited

To be held on Friday, May 5 at Walter Rabbit's tree stump at the edge of the Great Green Forest at 5pm

This meeting will address issue of consequence to all rabbits. Please come and bring all your friends and family

Fluffy Bunny on behalf of the Quest Team

This notice caused a flurry in the rabbit community and many conversations over ploughing the fields and picking vegetables. What was The Quest? Who was The Quest Team? What role did a young rabbit like Fluffy Bunny have and who was he to write

Fluffy Bunny is given the responsibility of putting up the notice for the community meeting

the notice? No information was forthcoming from any source. All Walter Rabbit would say was, "Come to the meeting and everything will be revealed."

Prior to this Walter Rabbit had met with Rominy Rabbit and prior to his meeting with Rominy Rabbit, Walter Rabbit had met with Rosemary Rabbit. Walter had opened his Rominy file and looked again at the list of Rominy Rabbit's likes and dislikes. He noted that Rominy liked Rosemary Rabbit and he felt that he could use this to his advantage in convincing Rominy Rabbit of the importance of The Quest whilst not upsetting Rominy Rabbit unduly.

He asked Rosemary Rabbit her opinion of Rominy Rabbit. Rosemary Rabbit eyed Walter Rabbit with some suspicion. "Why do you want to know?" she asked. "I feel it is time both of you thought about settling down and adding to the rabbit community," he said. "I know that Rominy Rabbit is attracted to you and I just wondered if there was any reciprocation?" "Oh," said Rosemary Rabbit, " if only it was so easy. Rominy Rabbit is sooooo handsome and he can have a great sense of humour, but why does he **always** have to be right! I don't know if I could live with someone who is completely one eyed. If only he could show some perspective, I would seriously consider your proposal."

"So," said Walter Rabbit, "what you are saying is that if it was possible to give Rominy Rabbit a degree of perspective that would make a difference. You may not believe this, but there might be a way. Make sure you come to the community meeting on Friday." Rosemary Rabbit said she wouldn't miss it and Walter Rabbit had his ammunition for his talk with Rominy Rabbit.

Walter Rabbit met with Rominy Rabbit over a cup of tea and some excellent turnip cakes (Rominy Rabbit's favourites) at Walter Rabbit's own burrow for privacy. After a general discussion and enquiries after Rominy Rabbit's family, Walter Rabbit moved to the future and Rominy Rabbit's hopes for a future with Rosemary Rabbit. Walter Rabbit listened to this carefully and then asked Rominy Rabbit how he believed Rosemary Rabbit felt about this. Rominy Rabbit sat silently for a little while and looked at his feet.

He then looked up at Walter Rabbit and said with a sigh. "She told me that she could never live with a one eyed rabbit and if I couldn't change, then she would not change her mind. But I don't feel one eyed. I have two perfectly good brown eyes and I don't know what to do!"

"The problem is related to carrots" said Walter. "Rabbits who eat carrots, see the world differently to those who don't eat any or eat few carrots."

"But carrots make me sick," cried Rominy Rabbit "and I come out in big spots." "I know that," replied Waler Rabbit, "but what if we could develop a tool that would help you see like the other rabbits, but without needing to eat carrots. What if we could discover the Carrot Effect?" "If that meant that Rosemary Rabbit would be my partner in life then anything would be worth it". said Rominy Rabbit. "Make sure you are at the meeting on Friday," said Walter Rabbit.

The Community Meeting on May 5 was the best ever attended in the history of the Happy Valley Rabbit Community. When Walter Rabbit stood on the tree stump at the edge of the Great Green Forest, he was amazed at the crowd that had gathered. Every family was represented and there were old and young rabbits, male and female rabbits and baby rabbits. Walter Rabbit was glad that he had prepared well and that he had a microphone. He raised his paw and the crowd of rabbits stilled to listen.

"My fellow rabbits," he said "I can't tell you how pleased I am to see this turnout. I want to discuss with you a very important issue that has arisen and to which we must find a solution. For the last week, I know you have been talking about The Quest and wondering what it is. Today is the day all will be revealed. But before I do this, I need to share some important information with you." Walter Rabbit explained about the data that he had collected about carrots and eyesight and thanked the rabbits who had helped him with this. The little rabbits, delighted to be acknowledged, jumped up and down with excitement. He then asked Fluffy Bunny and Reginald Rabbit to come to the front.

Reginald Rabbit had prepared a very large chart clearly

showing the results of this study and Fluffy Bunny was to present the results. The two rabbits held up the chart and Fluffy Bunny explained what it meant. "You will see," Fluffy Bunny said, "that if you eat 5 or more carrots a day, you have perfect eyesight, but that this decreases if you eat less than 5 carrots per day. You will see where Rominy Rabbit is on this chart as he eats no carrots!"

There was an audible gasp from the whole community as they realised how poor Rominy's eyesight was in relation to all of the other rabbits surveyed. Rominy was brought up close to look at the chart and his beautiful brown fur turned 3 shades lighter with shock. "As you know," Fluffy Bunny went on, "if your eyesight is bad, you have less perspective, so it is very hard to not only solve problems but also to identify problems. That means that you only see one solution and as you are aware, this can cause many problems and disrupt the harmony that usually exists in our community".

Fluffy Bunny could see everyone nodding in agreement and as Rominy Rabbit looked more and more sad, so he quickly handed over to Walter Rabbit again.

Walter Rabbit held up his paw again for silence. "I believe that we are obligated to try and solve this problem, to help both Rominy Rabbit and our whole community. I believe we need to search for The Carrot Effect that will improve eyesight and perspective in those rabbits that need it." A great cheer went up from the rabbit throng and it took some time for the noise to die down. "The search for the Carrot Effect will be The Quest and the search is to be undertaken by The Quest team. Could the team please step forward?"

Somewhat self-consciously Jenny Rabbit, Serena Rabbit and Quentin Rabbit joined Reginald Rabbit, Fluffy Bunny and Walter Rabbit at the front. Again a cheer went up and Walter Rabbit was pleased at the obvious support. Again he held up his paw. "We don't know how long The Quest for The Carrot Effect will take and we need your support to ensure things go on as normal while we are away. We want our team's families and employers to be supportive and for our team to retain their jobs and relationships. We also need a rabbit who can deputise for me on the tree stump and for nominations to be made in the next 24 hours." Walter Rabbit paused for effect. "Are there any questions or concerns?"

A variety of questions were asked including, how the team was chosen, where they were going to look, an estimate of the time they were going to be away, who was going to look after Jenny Rabbit's family and all of these were answered. Walter Rabbit then asked for a show of paws to indicate support and the support was unanimous. The Quest team looked at each other with relief. They were on their way!

The next day, Fluffy Bunny put up posters with the nominees for Tree Stump duties and the mechanism of voting. By the end of the week, Reginald Rabbit had added up all the votes and the clear leader was Sanderson Rabbit, the head gardener. Sanderson Rabbit and Walter Rabbit met to discuss his role and get a handover of outstanding issues and Walter Rabbit wished him good luck.

In the meantime, The Quest team had been preparing for their journey. They had decided what they needed, who would carry what and what sort of food to take. They just needed to agree on where to go. Where would they be most likely to find the Carrot Effect? Most of the team members believed they needed to go to where there was the most sunshine and space as that was where rabbits were most able to get perspective.

But Fluffy Bunny had a different idea. Fluffy Bunny felt it was important to go where it was most difficult to get perspective, because that was where The Carrot Effect was needed most and that was where it was most likely to be found. "If you can get perspective in a dark and enclosed place," he said "then you will be able to get perspective anywhere!" The team members looked at Fluffy Bunny and they suddenly knew why Walter Rabbit had selected him for the team. Reginald Rabbit held out his paw. "Put it there Fluffy Bunny," he said, "You have the makings of a future leader!" The other team members patted Fluffy Bunny on the back. They were going to the deepest, darkest part of the Great Green Forest.

Reginald Rabbit and Quentin Rabbit work together to fit all the pieces together

The Quest Team Sets Off

Two weeks after the community meeting, The Quest team set off. After many meetings and discussions, they felt comfortable with each other and excited about their task and the importance of this to the future of the rabbit community. Only Reginald Rabbit didn't carry a backpack, so as not to aggravate his arthritis and help him keep up with the others. Reginald Rabbit was in charge of the map of the Great Green Forest and the large watch for keeping time. Jenny Rabbit carried a folder for writing notes about anything that happened along the way. Quentin Rabbit was delegated the task of looking for clues that would point them in the direction of the Carrot Effect. Fluffy Bunny, the youngest and most energetic of the team, had the task of jumping on ahead and looking for opportunities and new paths. Serena Rabbit was to keep an eye out for wood creatures and make friendly overtures to them, so they would give them free passage. Walter Rabbit felt very satisfied with his team. They had started to work well together.

By the time they had reached the middle of the Great Green Forest it was evening and the rabbits decided to pitch camp and have some dinner. Everyone had an allotted task and by the time Reginald Rabbit's watch said 7PM, the tents were erected, dinner was cooked and a fire blazing. The rabbits were quiet as they ate their dinner and Walter Rabbit suggested that they should have a relaxing evening and review their plans in the morning.

Quentin Rabbit pulled out a large jigsaw puzzle that he had in his backpack and started putting this together. Reginald

Rabbit asked if he could assist and the young and old rabbit sat companionably next to each other finding pieces of jigsaw. Jenny Rabbit pulled out a huge book, saying that this was a rare opportunity to read. Fluffy Bunny still had huge amounts of energy, so he took a torch and went off to do some exploration. Serena Rabbit sat down next to Walter and probed him about the history of the rabbit clan.

The next morning after breakfast Walter Rabbit got his team together for some serious discussion. He pulled out a large sheet of paper from his backpack and attached it to a tree trunk with a small nail. On the top of the paper he had written:

DEFINING THE PROBLEM
Current Situation:

> ➢ There is a direct and inverse relationship between perspective and eating less than 5 carrots per day
> ➢ Lack of perspective causes major difficulty in identifying and solving problems
> ➢ If problems are not able to identified and effectively solved there will be continuing disharmony in the rabbit community

Desired Situation:

> ➢ The availability of a tool that will have the same effect as eating 5 or more carrots
> ➢ The outcome will be improved perspective in rabbits who eat less carrots and a harmonious rabbit community

Problem = Gap Between Current Situation and Desired Situation

"We need to find a useful tool, without knowing where it is, what it looks like or specifically where to find it (although we believe it is somewhere in the Great Green Forest)," said Walter Rabbit.

"How should we go about this process?"

The team looked at Walter who was silent. "What we need,"

said Walter Rabbit at last, "is data. Our team needs to divide up and gather relevant data from all sources. My suggestion is that Serena Rabbit interviews all the forest animals. I will work with Serena Rabbit to prepare an interview guide. Fluffy Bunny should explore to find opportunities and get ideas from the environment. Quentin Rabbit can explore in more detail to find clues that will contribute to the big picture. All data will be brought back each day and organised by Jenny Rabbit, then analysed by Reginald Rabbit. Is everyone agreeable to this and are there any other ideas?"

Reginald Rabbit raised his paw. "I think that data is imperative in our quest. I have been feeling that we have rushed off without a clear understanding of what we are looking for and although we have proof about perspective and its relationship to carrots, that is really all that we have. I really feel that we need quite a lot of data and this is likely to take us some weeks or even months! We shouldn't be impatient. Near enough is not good enough in trying to solve this problem which is critical for the future of our rabbit community. As well as analysing the data, I would also like to do some more detailed research into perspective itself."

Serena Rabbit said, "As part of our interviews of the forest animals, we should also use the eye chart that we used for our rabbit sample. Perhaps there may be some clues to perspective in the forest animals' diet or activities that we will be able to determine."

The team agreed that it was worthwhile pursuing these paths and a schedule was set. Data gathering activities would take place daily from 10 to 5. All of the data would be provided to Jenny Rabbit for organisation and once organised to Reginald Rabbit for analysis. At the end of four weeks, Reginald Rabbit would provide an initial report and a decision would then be made about whether there was sufficient data or whether more needed to be collected.

The rabbits had an exceptionally busy few weeks. Fluffy Bunny, roamed through many miles of the Great Green Forest and on one occasion even emerged out the other side. He wrote short notes in his little notebook and every evening tore out the pages to give to Jenny Rabbit.

Quentin Rabbit surveyed the environment in much more detail. He didn't go very far but he searched for clues on the ground, in the trees, in plants and streams and behind rocks. Each time he noted a clue he packed it into his backpack and every evening he emptied his backpack and provided the contents to Jenny Rabbit.

Serena Rabbit and Walter Rabbit prepared an interview guide for the forest animals. Serena Rabbit conducted the interviews then sent the forest animals on to Walter Rabbit who had set the Eye Chart up in a small glade. Each evening they provided their results to Jenny Rabbit.

Reginald Rabbit spent the first few says researching "perspective" and then began to work on analysing the data that Jenny Rabbit had organised.

At the end of the four weeks, Reginald Rabbit and Jenny Rabbit were still working on organising and analysing, so the rest of the team, decided there was an opportunity for a big cook up and a clean up, so everyone was still gainfully occupied. This resulted in a wonderful dinner on Sunday night, by which time Reginald and Jenny Rabbit had finished their work and were able to relax. "Tomorrow," said Walter Rabbit, will be a day off. So eat well and sleep as long as you like. On Tuesday, we will have a look at our data and see what we can glean". The rabbits cheered. They all felt pleased with their achievements so far.

The Team Reviews The Data

On Tuesday morning the team felt refreshed and ready to recommence their task. Walter handed over to Jenny Rabbit to explain how she had organised the data first and then to Reginald Rabbit to discuss the analysis.

Jenny Rabbit explained how she had added up the results of the surveys and put the comments together. Then she explained how she used all of the information from the other members of the team to develop a set of themes that seemed similar.

Reginald Rabbit then discussed what he had learnt about "perspective" and what he had gleaned from the data.

I looked up in the Oxford dictionary, the meaning of "perspective", he said. "There are a number of meanings, and all have some degree of relevance to our Quest."

Perspective: *1* a view or prospect. *2* a particular way of regarding something. *3* understanding of the relative importance of things.

If we look at **1** a view or prospect: this relates to being able to see the whole picture, as far as the eye can see. It conjures up a feeling of openness and space and being receptive to new ideas.

"I love to get up high," said Fluffy Bunny. "It's amazing what you can see if you climb a tree. I can see when all the humans have left the fields and its safe to take some more carrots." Reginald Rabbit frowned and went on:

"If we look at **2** a particular way of regarding something: this can give us the opposite effect. Using this definition, it reminds us that our minds may be closed to all other ways of looking at things as we can only see things in one way. It is good to hold an opinion, but not to the exclusion of not being able to see others points of view."

Walter Rabbit sighed. "You have exactly described Rominy Rabbit. He only ever has one point of view. Just thinking about it gives me a headache!" Reginald Rabbit nodded his head:

"If we look at **3** understanding of the relative importance of things: this gives us a feeling that we can assess priorities amongst a number of options, so that we can logically choose what is best, generally using appropriate data and establishing parameters or boundaries."

Quentin Rabbit said, "I use this principle in putting together jigsaw puzzles. I find the bits that stand out and build parts of the picture around them."

"Well," said Reginald Rabbit, it seems these definitions may in fact be very useful as we move forward."

Reginald Rabbit then pulled out some charts and attached these to the surrounding trees. He cleared his throat. "Harrumph," he said, clearing his throat. "You will see that there is a lot of data, but I am not sure what it tells us or how much it helps The Quest, but I am sure that together we can make some sense of it."

Sheet one showed the results of the survey. Serena Rabbit had been very busy and had managed to interview 30 different small forest animals. All of these had had their eyesight reviewed by Walter Rabbit.

"You will note," said Reginald Rabbit, "that none of these animals eat carrots, but that all have good eyesight. The animals all have a diet of roots and berries, shoots and leaves that are readily available in the Great Green Forest. You will also note that animals that eat a larger proportion of a certain type of berry seem to have better eyesight. I don't know how this helps us, but what it does show is that these berries have a sort of a Carrot Effect."

"Perhaps we could add these berries to the diet of our problem rabbits to mimic carrots?" suggested Serena Rabbit. "Are we sure they aren't poisonous for rabbits?" asked Quentin Rabbit. "I never get sick," said Fluffy Bunny. "I would be prepared to try a few and see if I can digest them".

"We are not into solutions yet!" said Reginald Rabbit sternly. "Looking at only a part of the data is almost as bad as collecting no data. Before we look at how to use this data, we need to look at the rest. Jenny Rabbit has put together the data gathered by Fluffy Bunny and Quentin Rabbit into a number of lists."

List One

Pathways

- ➤ Path from our campsite leading to a very tall pine tree
- ➤ Long curving path leading out of the Great Green Forest
- ➤ Stream in middle of the Great Green Forrest leads to a waterfall
- ➤ Most berries grow under the tallest trees and along the paths
- ➤ Some animals eat insects
- ➤ A large pine tree with branches for easy climbing

List Two

Colours

- ➤ Pine cones with orange colouring under the tree
- ➤ Large orange flowers bordered the end of the path
- ➤ Ducks with orange bellies swimming in the stream
- ➤ Berries range from red to black in colour
- ➤ Some insects are an orange colour
- ➤ The flame tree has multicoloured leaves

List Three

Consequences

- ➤ Pine cone fell on Fluffy Bunny's head and he saw orange stars
- ➤ Flowers had a strange smell
- ➤ Ducks flew in formation when they left the water

> ➤ Animals that eat black berries see best in the dark
> ➤ An insect diet has no relationship to eyesight
> ➤ The view from the pine tree is amazing

"Did you climb the Pine Tree Fluffy Bunny?" asked Serena Rabbit. "Yes I did," replied Fluffy Bunny. "I could see all the way to Happy Valley in one direction and all the way to the mountains in the other direction". "Was it difficult?" asked Quentin Rabbit. "Not really," replied Fluffy Bunny. "The branches are very close together and I could jump from branch to branch. I am sure if we could get up there we would gain a group perspective."

"You are still trying to get solutions—**NO SOLUTIONS**!" said Reginald Rabbit. "We must explore the data from all angles first".

The team looked at the data for a long time and at last Reginald Rabbit stood up again and put forward his views.

"This data shows us a number of things if we get away from the detail and focus on what the data represents. Let's start with our original problem and try to get some of our own perspective".

Current Situation:
> ➤ There is a direct and inverse relationship between perspective and eating less than 5 carrots per day
> ➤ Lack of perspective causes major difficulty in identifying and solving problems
> ➤ If problems are not able to identified and effectively solved there will be continuing disharmony in the rabbit community

Desired Situation:
> ➤ The availability of a tool that will have the same effect as eating 5 or more carrots
> ➤ The outcome will be improved perspective in rabbits who eat less carrots and a harmonious rabbit community

Problem = Gap Between Current Situation and Desired Situation

"How do we develop a suitable and simple tool to improve perspective and problem identification and problem solving ability in myopic rabbits?"

"Let's think of this as an equation," said Reginald Rabbit. "Remember, Rominy Rabbit loves equations and if we can devise something that looks like an equation it has a high likelihood of improving Rominy Rabbit's problem with perception."

Quentin Rabbit jumped up. "I can think of an equation," he cried. Quentin Rabbit took a clean sheet of paper and attached it to a tree. On the sheet of paper he drew a diagram.

Improving Problem Identification and Solution	
Increase Perspective	**Decrease Reliance On Eyes**
Eat more carrots	Use brain instead of eyes
Eat black berries	Use ears
Rise above the problem	Listen to other people
Write problems as equations	Brightly light the path
	Put coloured signs along the way

The equation is:

Increased perspective + decreased reliance on eyesight = improved problem identification and solution

"I think that this would work for many problems," went on Quentin Rabbit excitedly as he wrote a hypothetical problem up on his paper.

Current Situation:
- ➢ Stock of carrots running down
- ➢ Good supply of turnips and apples
- ➢ At this rate there may not be enough appropriate food for winter

Desired Situation:
- ➢ Increased stock of carrots to ensure at least 5 carrots per rabbit per day
- ➢ Overall stock of vegetables enough for winter with some to spare

Problem:

How to improve our food stocks to ensure adequate appropriate food for winter.

Equation:

Increased food stocks + decreased consumption = adequate appropriate food for winter

Increase Food Stocks	Decrease Consumption
Plant more carrots	Keep food locked up to prevent stealing
Plant more turnips and sweet corn	Limit carrots to a maximum of 5 per day indefinitely
Gather more apples	Promote eating of other more plentiful food
Build more storage facilities	

Quentin Rabbit stopped writing and turned to the team. "I think this equation will work whenever there is a problem related to demand and supply and many of our problems relate to this. What do you think?" he asked breathlessly.

There was considerable laughter and discussion as each rabbit nominated problems that could be identified and solved using this tool.

Finally Reginald Rabbit stood and raised his paw. "What I want to know is, how will this help Rominy Rabbit and all of the other rabbits that have poor perspective and are somewhat one-eyed?"

Walter Rabbit had been quiet through this whole exchange and had listened with interest to the discussions amongst the team. He was starting to feel that there was some light at the end of the tunnel and that perhaps a solution was being discovered.

"I think that we are getting somewhere." said Walter Rabbit. "But we need to be very careful. Firstly we should be sure that our solution is not too complex and secondly that we don't expect our tool to work in every situation. After all it is just a tool. I can see that this will work in some situations, but not in others, so we have only come up with part of the solution."

He searched in his Rominy Rabbit file and found the list that he had originally developed with Rominy Rabbit's likes and dislikes. He attached this sheet to a tree. "Do you see any solutions in this?" he asked. The team examined the sheet and Quentin Rabbit jumped up. "There are some definite clues in this list," and he quickly drew a diagram.

The diagram was pieces of a jigsaw puzzle with bits of a picture on each.

"Here are parts of a whole picture," said Quentin Rabbit. "If we can devise an equation to solve problems, get Rominy Rabbit to use the technique, show Rosemary Rabbit that he is capable of change and reward him in the short term with his favourite vegetables, we will end up with a happy Rominy Rabbit who will sing all day long!"

Quentin Rabbit quickly interlocked the pieces and there was a happy and singing Rominy Rabbit. "This is the whole picture," said Quentin Rabbit.

The team nodded in agreement and Fluffy Bunny jumped up excitedly. "I think this needs to be part of a bigger picture so that we can see the impact on the whole rabbit community. But we need and rely more on our brains than our eyes to see the rest of the picture. In addition, we need to have better light and signposting so that the whole picture is revealed. Walter Rabbit, we need to rise above the problem to see the whole picture. I really think we must go to the top of the tall pine to get both our own perspective and a group perspective!"

Reginald Rabbit and Serena Rabbit looked most unhappy with this suggestion. Reginald Rabbit complained that he was too old and arthritic to climb trees. Serena Rabbit stated that she was afraid to climb trees after a disastrous climbing accident in her youth.

"How far away is the tall pine?" asked Walter Rabbit. "I suppose it would take us the best part of a day with all of our gear", replied Fluffy Bunny. "Well", said Walter Rabbit, "supposing we ignore our issues with climbing. If this is not a problem, do we agree as a team that we need to get above the problem and rely more on our brains, better light and signposting to find our solution?"

The team agreed that this made sense. "My suggestion is," said Walter Rabbit, "that we make the trek to the tall pine and have a look at the possibilities when we get there. We can then see if there are other options available to us to rise above the problem. Is everyone happy with this approach?"

The team agreed to this suggestion and the next day they packed up their campsite and followed Fluffy Bunny down the path to the tall pine.

The Team Gains Perspective

It was evening by the time they reached the tall pine. The tall pine stood in a clearing. Underneath were orange tinted pinecones and many bushes with black berries. Just beyond the tall pine was a sparkling stream in which swam the orange-bellied ducks and around the edges of the clearing grew large orange flowers. The team stared in wonderment. The solution had to be here. Despite their long hike, they suddenly felt refreshed and uplifted. There was a sense of euphoria in the air.

Walter Rabbit looked at his team. He could see that their thoughts were as one. Each knew what the other was thinking. He gazed up above the tall pine, where he could see the sun setting, its rays filtering through the greenery. Just then the orange bellied ducks spread their wings and lifted themselves gracefully out of the stream. They flew in formation over the tall pine showing their orange bellies to those watching below.

This is an omen; Walter Rabbit thought to himself. Tomorrow will be the day. Then he said it out loud. The team looked at Walter Rabbit and all said together. "Tomorrow will be the day!"

Walter Rabbit was woken by the sunlight streaming in through the flap of his tent. He gazed through the tent flap and in the bright sunlight everything was clear. The tall pine stood proudly. A few small forest animals were eating the black berries and beyond the tall pine Walter could see something that made him stare in surprise and bound outside. There in the clearing

Flyer Rabbit takes Fluffy Bunny and the rest of the team on a perspective finding trip

was a gigantic hot air balloon. The canopy was bright orange with a green top. In fact it looked like an enormous carrot!

In Walter Rabbit's head a phrase kept repeating itself. "**Today** is the day. Today **is** the day. Today is the **day**." He had an enormous sense of excitement and anticipation.

No-one else had yet stirred, so Walter Rabbit approached the hot air balloon and looked inside. He surprised a large black rabbit wearing aviator goggles and a hat. "Morning old fella," said the black rabbit. "Not so much of the old," said Walter Rabbit. "Good morning to you. I am Walter Rabbit". "Apologies for any offence," replied the black rabbit. "Flyer Rabbit at your service".

"How did you know where to find us?" asked Walter Rabbit? "Now that would be telling." replied Flyer Rabbit. "Suffice to say that I did and here I am. Where's the rest of the crew?" Walter Rabbit said he would wake them and asked Flyer Rabbit to share their breakfast. With no second invitation, Flyer Rabbit hopped out of the balloon and went to put on the kettle.

The team was amazed and fascinated by the hot air balloon and by Flyer Rabbit. Fluffy Bunny could barely contain his excitement and needed to be held back by Flyer Rabbit as he tried to climb into the balloon basket. "Listen young fella," he said. This isn't a toy. I'll show you everything when we get underway, but until then you will eat your breakfast with the rest of us and be patient!"

Chastened, Fluffy Bunny did as he was told, but could not help himself from looking longingly at the hot air balloon from time to time. He suddenly knew what he wanted to do in life and how to channel his adventurous spirit into a real career.

"We now have all of the elements for our solution," said Walter Rabbit, as they tidied up after breakfast.

- ➤ "A great team working in harmony
- ➤ A way to rise above our problem
- ➤ A balloon that looks like a gigantic carrot
- ➤ Excellent sunlight to light our way
- ➤ Signposting provided by the tall pine and the stream
- ➤ A facilitator to assist us with the solution in Flyer Rabbit."

"And a fantastic leader," added Jenny Rabbit. "Here, here," said the rest of the team.

"So let's go already," said Fluffy Bunny, unable to contain himself any longer and he and Flyer Rabbit jumped into the basket together. Fluffy Bunny watched carefully as Flyer Rabbit prepared the hot air balloon for flight, asking questions and helping where he could. The other rabbits held on to the sides and gazed up at the canopy. Serena Rabbit looked apprehensive and Jenny Rabbit gently held her paw and talked to her softly. Quentin Rabbit examined the clearing from all angles, still searching for clues and Reginald Rabbit thought back to his youth, sighed and wished he was young again.

Slowly the balloon began to rise, up over the clearing, up towards the top of the tall pine until at last it hung over the tall pine and the clearing, suspended in space. Everything below looked very small, but the overall effect was of a large painting with different colours and textures divided by strips of white, the paths and roads, rather like a complex jigsaw puzzle that had been cleverly put together. Quentin Rabbit sighed. "If only I could paint, then I could design new jigsaw puzzles."

Walter Rabbit gazed at the earth below and how it met the sky at the horizon. "How can we provide this majestic viewpoint to Rominy Rabbit and other rabbits with poor eyesight?" he asked the team. It was Jenny Rabbit who replied. "It seems so obvious up here," she said. "It shows us how the whole is larger than the sum of its parts." "Yes," agreed Quentin Rabbit." When you are doing a jigsaw puzzle it really means nothing until you have the whole picture. You spend a lot of time putting similar pieces in piles for parts of the puzzle, then joining them together and all the preparation is very important, as this gives you the signposts along the way, but the solution is the whole puzzle and when you have the whole puzzle you have—I can only call it –ART!"

"I can identify with ART," cried Serena Rabbit, "and solving problems successfully really is an art."

The hot air balloon floated peacefully across the sky and as the rabbits looked down, they noticed that they were hovering over Happy Valley. They could see Farmer Brown's fields and the large vegetable garden and the Big Bunny Café with its bright blue flag. Suddenly they all felt a bit homesick. "Do you want to land?" asked Flyer Rabbit. The team all nodded yes, but Walter Rabbit sighed and said, "We are not quite finished and we do need to complete our solution at the tall pine. The good news is that I think we are nearly done and we will be going home very soon. We must get our job done properly before we go back home."

So Flyer Rabbit turned the Balloon back towards the tall pine in the Great Green Forest and the rabbits all held each others paws as they touched down to indicate their understanding of their homesickness and the need to complete the solution.

In the morning all the team was up early. They were eager to go home and knew that before this was possible, they needed to finish The Quest. They wanted to start on their conclusions as soon as possible and not waste another minute.

Walter Rabbit stood up. "I understand exactly how you feel. I miss home and Amelia Rabbit intensely, but we have spent many weeks away. We just need one or two more days to work together on tying up the loose ends. We need to re-energise and finish our task. Just like yesterday, we need to look at the big picture. The right solution will provide harmony and happiness in our rabbit community and as a spin off, happiness and a sense of achievement for all of us as individuals." Just then the orange bellied ducks swooped out of the sky and settled in the stream. "Yes we can do this and we will," thought all members of the team as one.

"Imagine that I am Rominy Rabbit", said Walter Rabbit. "I have come to you not with a problem. but with a solution. Let's pretend that this solution is that I deserve more turnips as I don't eat carrots. How will you use the data we have to convince me that there is an underlying problem, that there are options to solve the problem and that some options are better than others?"

"Do we have to use **all** of the data we have?" asked Jenny Rabbit. "That's a very perceptive question," replied Walter Rabbit.

"I think we will find that some of the data is more important and we will need to use both our judgement and our team skills to sift through the data and use what is key to our task. This includes everything we know about Rominy Rabbit himself."

The team prepared the following list in answer to Walter Rabbit's question:

➢ What would convince Rominy to think of things differently – the "What's in it for me" question? For Rominy it would be having Rosemary Rabbit as a partner

➢ Talk in terms he can understand- Rominy doesn't understand the term "the big picture", so we need to talk in terms of Rabbit community- his friends and neighbours that he has to live with day after day. This is what the term 'big picture' really means to us

➢ Get him to pretend he is one of the other rabbits and see it from the other rabbit's point of view- eg Jenny Rabbit and her large family, how would implementing his solution affect Jenny's family and affect how Jenny feels about Rominy and his solution. Rominy wouldn't want Jenny's family to miss out on their turnips and be hungry

➢ Once he sees why he should do it, give him a structure so that he will see all problems in terms of the current situation and the desired situation. So Rominy needs to list all of the things that are bothering him at present relating to this issue and the impact on other rabbits. He should then visualise (using his brain rather than eyes) all of the things he would like to see if the problem was fixed. He needs to have a list for each. We can help him with the list

➢ Once that happens he has an equation: Increase in factors that make up desired situation - decrease in factors that make up current situation = elimination of problem

➢ Then he can work out all the things that contribute to both sides of the equation so the current situation factors get smaller and the desired situation factors get larger.

> ➤ After that he needs to decide which of these factors will be the best to do and likely to achieve the best result
> ➤ Then he needs to develop strategies for each selected factor

"Of course," said Jenny Rabbit, in our structure we will need to consider that understanding the point of view of other rabbits is one mechanism, but that some problems are best solved by using a team of rabbits that will understand all aspects of the problem. So another step would be to decide if a team is needed to provide a better solution."

"And," added Reginald Rabbit, "it will be important to collect some data, so that Rominy Rabbit can evaluate his success in solving the problem." The group nodded. As they were talking Walter Rabbit had written a list.

Problem solving techniques for myopic rabbits (or for anyone who needs help solving problems)

> ➤ Appeal to the rabbit's specific needs to get them to listen to a new way of doing things. (so we need to identify these needs first)
> ➤ Communicate in language that the rabbit will understand
> ➤ Get into the shoes of others affected by the problem or solution proposed
> ➤ Think about all of the issues that are of concern now (current situation) and what you think a successful solution will deliver (desired situation)
> ➤ Write up the equation: Increase in factors that make up desired situation—decrease in factors that make up current situation=elimination of problem
> ➤ Decide whether a team would get a better solution (for more complex problems or those that affect many rabbits). Choose an appropriate team if necessary
> ➤ Work on the factors in both Current situation and Desired situation to decrease or eliminate the Problem.
> ➤ Decide which of these factors are likely to be the best to work on and give results.

> ➢ Develop strategies for each of the chosen elements
> ➢ Evaluate degree of success

Fluffy Bunny had a concerned look on his face. "I'm not quite sure how we decide on which of the factors to work on," he said.

"I think, we need to develop some constraints to help do this," answered Quentin Rabbit. We need to draw a table with headings and assess each factor against the headings".

"But what should the headings be?" asked Fluffy Bunny again.

"Things like:
> ➢ how easy will it be to do,
> ➢ how much time will it take,
> ➢ how practical is it to work on,
> ➢ how much will it cost,"

replied Quentin Rabbit. "If it's going to take too long or be too costly or too hard, we seriously have to consider whether this is the best solution."

"And with a good team", added Jenny Rabbit, "we will be able to decide these things in an organised way."

"To make it even simpler," said Quentin Rabbit, "I think we could show how our problem will get smaller on a diagram."

Quentin Rabbit pulled a large sheet of paper out of his backpack and drew some lines on it.

"I think we now really have a tool that will deliver us The Carrot Effect," said Walter Rabbit. "This tool will effectively improve short-sightedness and enable myopic rabbits gain perspective by using their brains rather than their eyes. Now we just need to test it on Rominy Rabbit and I don't think that this will be difficult. He is sure to have some issue right now that needs attending to."

"And," said Serena Rabbit, "I suggest once Rominy Rabbit successfully uses the Carrot Effect we reward him with a stock of turnips and lettuce for winter." All the team agreed that this was a good idea.

The rest of the day was spent making preparations. The journey out of the Great Green Forest would take two days as they would camp overnight at their original camp site.

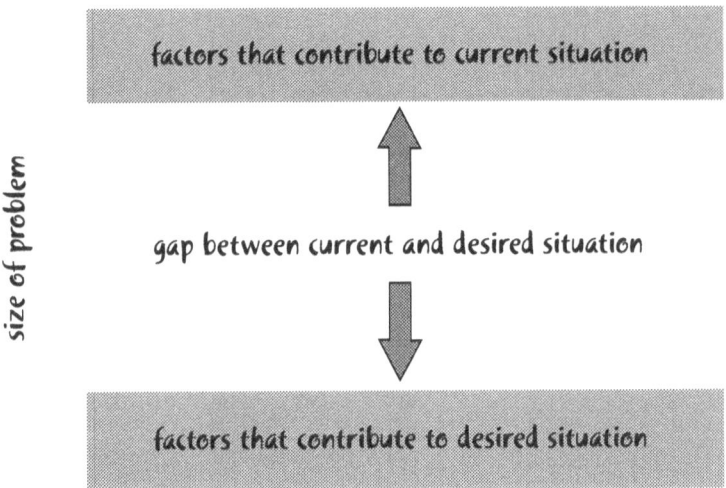

Jenny Rabbit and Serena Rabbit relax after a successful quest

The Team Heads For Home

The rabbits were quiet as they headed back on the first day. It was as if all of their work had caught up with them and they had no energy or brainpower left except to walk. Fluffy Bunny still hopped, but even he was somewhat subdued. Their great adventure was over and their team had completed its task. Walter Rabbit was deep in thought on the way back. How should he reward and acknowledge his team? They had worked so hard and had given up considerable time to be part of The Quest.

He knew only too well that if he didn't do this effectively, there could be a degree of unhappiness and discontent. Slowly an idea formed itself in his mind. There would be an "event" to promote The Carrot Effect and at this event each team member would be publicly acknowledged for their part both verbally and with a special orange and green certificate.

When they made camp for the night, Walter Rabbit presented the event idea to the team. The team brightened up considerably in response to this discussion and decided to set up an event meeting on their return with the big event to be scheduled one week later. This event would launch The Carrot Effect to the Happy Valley Rabbit Community.

The rest of the evening was spent in relaxation. Jenny Rabbit pulled out her large book again. Serena Rabbit worked on her tapestry.

Reginald Rabbit and Quentin Rabbit completed the jigsaw puzzle they had commenced at the start of The Quest. "It's funny," remarked Quentin Rabbit, "that the jigsaw puzzle seems easier to do now doesn't it?" "Yes," agreed Reginald Rabbit. "I have found that it is really useful to leave some time between trying to solve a problem and completing the solution. The brain seems to revitalise and everything falls into place much more easily." "We probably should add this to our problem solving rules," said Quentin Rabbit. "Sit on the problem for a while before coming up with the final solution."

Fluffy Bunny thought about his new career and the discussions he had had with Flyer Rabbit in the hot air balloon. And Walter Rabbit thought about Amelia Rabbit, a nice hot bath and his favourite soup.

The trek back home was livelier. The rabbits chatted to each other and Fluffy Bunny hopped ahead as usual then came back to report on where they were. As they emerged from the Great Green Forest into the sunlight, they saw rabbits come forward from all the surrounding fields and the rabbits formed a guard of honour for the team as they headed for home.

There was much jubilation in the Happy Valley Rabbit Community that night as families welcomed their loved ones. Sounds of happy rabbit chatter and laughter were heard into the night. Many carrots were consumed in a variety of dishes, songs were sung and Jenny Rabbit's children danced energetically around the washing line until they fell down exhausted.

Later that evening as Walter Rabbit sat quietly finishing his favourite soup, there was a knock on the door. Amelia Rabbit opened the door and there stood Rominy Rabbit looking rather nervous. "Come in" Said Amelia Rabbit. "Has something upset you?" "Oh Amelia Rabbit, I just have to know- did Walter Rabbit find it? Did he find The Carrot Effect?"

Walter Rabbit stood up from his chair and gave Rominy Rabbit his paw. "Yes Rominy Rabbit, we found The Carrot Effect and tomorrow you will be the first to try it out!"

Rominy Rabbit beamed from ear to ear. He was indeed a very handsome rabbit when he smiled. Tomorrow was the beginning of a new era. He knew that he would be successful and he could hardly wait!

The Team celebrates their success

The Carrot Effect

This story is about solving complex problems and how to overcome barriers that are put in the way.

It is about good leadership, epitomised in Walter Rabbit, the wise, courageous, experienced and respected leader who knows he can't do it on his own and is prepared to take risks for the greater good.

It is about teamwork and choosing the right team to achieve an outcome with different and diverse personalities and skills that may not be easily identified.

It is about lack of perspective or shortsightedness and how this can be cured by gaining appropriate insight symbolised by carrots.

It is about preparation and collecting data and **no solutions** until appropriate data has been collected and analysed.

It is about risk taking, exploration, persistence, and having fun in search of the outcome.

Finally it is about the importance of acknowledging and rewarding the efforts of your team once the task is completed.

My hope is that you will be entertained and that you will find some small idea that you can use in your own life.